Spanish for Travelers

A Practical Guide

Daria Gałek

While every precaution has been taken in the preparation of this book, the publisher assumes no responsibility for errors or omissions, or for damages resulting from the use of the information contained herein.

SPANISH FOR TRAVELERS: A PRACTICAL GUIDE

First edition. July 28, 2023.

ISBN: 979-8223562283

Written by Daria Gałek.

Table of Contents

Introduction

"Spanish for Travelers" is a practical guide designed specifically for people who are planning to travel to a Spanish–speaking country or want to communicate freely during their foreign trips. The book includes useful vocabulary and phrases that are essential in typical travel situations. You will find sample sentences that will help you ask for directions, place an order at a restaurant, make accommodation reservations, and much more. The book also provides practical tips on how to use Spanish in various travel situations, how to avoid common mistakes, and how to gain confidence in communication.

"Spanish for Travelers" is an excellent aid for travelers who want to master the basics of the Spanish language and communicate effortlessly in a Spanish–speaking environment during their adventures abroad. I hope this book will be helpful to you and enable you to communicate confidently during your travels!

Chapter 1: Basic Phrases and Questions

Welcome to the first chapter of our practical guide, "Spanish for Travelers"! This chapter is dedicated to the most essential basic phrases and questions that will help you communicate in a Spanish-speaking environment during your travels.

Learning these phrases and questions is crucial as they enable you to make the first contact with locals, waiters, guides, or fellow travelers. They will make you feel more confident in an unfamiliar environment and help you adapt to a new setting.

In this chapter, you will find basic polite expressions such as "good morning," "please," "thank you," "excuse me," which are essential for everyday interactions. You will also learn how to introduce yourself and ask for names and origins.

Remember that understanding these simple expressions is the first step towards opening up to new cultures and gaining unforgettable experiences while traveling. Whether you are in Spain, Mexico, or any other Spanish-speaking destination, knowing these phrases will help you fully enjoy your journey.

We invite you to learn and practice these basic phrases and questions! Ready? *¡Vamos! (Let's begin!)*

Basic Courtesy Forms and Greetings

In the Spanish language, there are several courtesy forms used depending on the social context and the level of familiarity with the interlocutor. It is essential to familiarize yourself with them to express respect and politeness in various situations, whether interacting with strangers or close acquaintances.

Learning these basic courtesy forms and greetings will allow you to make a positive first impression and communicate more easily in a new environment. Remember that politeness and courtesy are significant elements in Spanish–speaking countries, so it's important to use these phrases correctly.

1. Courtesy Pronouns

In the Spanish language, there are two main courtesy pronouns:

– "usted" – used to address one person formally. It corresponds to the English "sir" or "ma'am."

– "ustedes" – used to address a group of people formally. It corresponds to the English "ladies and gentlemen."

Example sentences:

– *¿Cómo está usted? – How are you, sir/ma'am?*

– *¿Qué desean ustedes? – What do you ladies and gentlemen wish?*

Using these courtesy forms will help you create a positive and respectful impression in Spanish–speaking environments.

2. Greetings

In the Spanish language, like in other languages, greetings are an important element of social communication. By expressing a polite greeting, we establish the first contact with another person and show them respect and friendliness. In Spanish–speaking countries, there are various greetings used at different times of the day and depending on the social context.

The most common greetings are:

– *Hola* – *Hello / Hi* (informal greeting)

– *Buenos días* – *Good morning* (greeting in the morning)

– *Buenas tardes* – *Good afternoon* (greeting in the afternoon)

– *Buenas noches* – *Goodnight / Good evening* (greeting in the evening or before sleep)

Additionally, you can use one of the following expressions to greet someone:

– *¿Qué tal?* – *How are you? / How's it going?*

– *¿Cómo estás?* – *How are you?*

– *¿Cómo te va?* – *How's it going for you?*

– *¿Cómo andas?* – *How are you doing?*

– *¿Qué pasa?* – *What's up? / What's happening?*

– *¿Cómo has estado?* – *How have you been?* (more formal)

– *¿Cómo le va?* – *How are you?* (polite way to address an older person or someone you don't know well)

3. Introducing Yourself

Using appropriate polite forms when introducing yourself in Spanish is important, especially in business meetings, formal situations, and conversations with older individuals or authorities. The right expressions and pronouns used during introductions help to show respect and courtesy towards the other person.

Here are a few examples of how we can introduce ourselves in Spanish, using polite forms:

– *Me llamo Ana. ¿Y usted?* – *My name is Ana. And you?*

In this polite form, "usted" is used with older individuals, authorities, clients, or strangers. It is a way to express respect and politeness.

– *Soy el señor López. Mucho gusto.* – *I am Mr. López. Nice to meet you.*

In this case, we use the form "el señor" or "la señora" (Mr./Mrs.) before the last name, which is a more formal way of introducing oneself.

Remember that when introducing yourself in Spanish, we have the option to choose between the informal pronoun "tú" (you) or the formal "usted" (you) depending on the context and situation. In less formal, friendly situations, we can use "tú," while in more formal or unfamiliar contacts, it is better to use "usted."

During introductions, it's also good to pay attention to polite expressions, such as:

– *Mucho gusto* – *Nice to meet you*

– *Encantado/a* – *Pleased to meet you, with pleasure*

– *Agradable conocerle* – *Nice to meet you* (formal)

Using these expressions during conversations helps to create a positive impression and express respect towards the other person.

4. Addressing Other People

Using the appropriate polite pronouns is crucial during conversations with other people in Spanish. The proper use of pronouns allows us to express respect, courtesy, and tact in our interactions with others.

Here are a few examples of how we can use polite pronouns in different situations:

– *¿Puedo ayudarle en algo, señor?* – *Can I help you with something, sir/ma'am?*

– *¿Tienen ustedes alguna pregunta?* – *Do you have any questions?*

– *Perdone, ¿tiene usted un momento?* – *Excuse me, do you have a moment?*

– *¿Cómo se encuentra, señor Martínez?* – *How are you, Mr. Martínez?*

5. Ending the Conversation

During the conclusion of a conversation, we use polite expressions to express gratitude or bid farewell. Using the appropriate expressions can leave a positive impression on our interlocutors. Here are a few simple phrases that will help you end the conversation politely:

– *¡Gracias!* – *Thank you!*

– *Que tenga un buen día.* – *Have a nice day.*

– *Adiós.* – *Goodbye.*

– *Hasta la próxima.* – *Until next time.*

– *Muchas gracias por su ayuda.* – *Thank you very much for your help.*

– *Hasta luego.* – *See you later.*

– *Cuídate.* – *Take care.*

– *Nos vemos mañana.* – *See you tomorrow.*

– *¡Buen viaje!* – *Have a good trip!*

– *Hasta pronto.* – *See you soon.*

Questions about Name, Origin, and Purpose of the Trip

During your travels to Spanish–speaking countries, you will often want to initiate contact with local residents. Questions about name, origin, and purpose of the trip are essential elements of any conversation. Now, you will learn how to ask these questions politely and how to respond to them.

1. Questions about Name

To ask someone's name, you can use the following expressions:

– *¿Cómo te llamas?* – *What's your name?* (informal)

– *¿Cómo se llama usted?* – *What's your name?* (formal)

– *¿Cuál es tu nombre?* – *What's your name?* (informal)

Responses to these questions:

– *Me llamo María.* – *My name is Maria.*

– *Soy Carlos.* – *I am Carlos.*

– *Mi nombre es Ana.* – *My name is Ana.*

2. Questions about Origin

If you want to find out where someone comes from, you can ask the following questions:

– *¿De dónde eres?* – *Where are you from?* (informal)

– ¿De dónde es usted? – Where are you from? (formal)

– ¿De qué país eres? – Which country are you from?

– ¿De dónde vienes? – Where do you come from?

– ¿Cuál es tu nacionalidad? – What is your nationality?

– ¿En qué ciudad naciste? – In which city were you born?

– ¿Dónde creciste? – Where did you grow up?

Possible responses:

– Soy de Reino Unido. – I am from United Kingdom.

– Soy de Londres. – I am from London.

– Vengo de Nueva York. – I come from New York.

– Mi nacionalidad es estadounidense. – My nationality is American.

– Nací en Chicago. – I was born in Chicago.

– Crecí en Washington. – I grew up in Washington.

3. Questions about the purpose of the trip

During a conversation with other travelers or locals, you can ask about the purpose of their trip. Here are a few examples of questions:

– ¿Cuál es el propósito de tu viaje? – What is the purpose of your trip? (informal)

– ¿Cuál es el propósito de su viaje? – What is the purpose of your trip? (formal)

– ¿Para qué estás aquí? – What are you here for?

– ¿A qué has venido? – What have you come for?

Possible answers:

– Voy de vacaciones. – I am going on vacation.

– Estoy aquí por negocios. – I am here for business.

– Vengo a conocer la cultura local. – I came to experience the local culture.

– Estoy de paso hacia otro destino. – I am passing through to another destination.

– Vamos a visitar a nuestros familiares. – We are visiting our relatives.

Remember to maintain politeness and respect when asking these questions. Use appropriate courtesy pronouns and polite language to express your courtesy in the conversation. With these simple phrases, you'll be able to easily connect with others during your travels and learn more about them.

Tips for Pronunciation and Accent

Correct pronunciation is a crucial element of effective communication in Spanish. However, for learners of this language, it can be challenging as some sounds and accents may differ from those in their native language. It is essential, therefore, to understand the basic rules of pronunciation in Spanish to better navigate the learning process.

1. Pay attention to the pronunciation of letters

The pronunciation of letters is a crucial element in learning Spanish. In most cases, letters are pronounced unambiguously, which makes learning and communication easier. However, it's worth noting some specific sounds that may pose challenges.

The letter "r" and double "rr" are two sounds that often present difficulties for Spanish learners. The "r" sound is pronounced slightly harder and more accentuated than in Polish. The double "rr," on the other hand, is known as the trilled or rolled "r," which is produced by vibrating the tongue against the palate. To master these sounds, it's helpful to practice their pronunciation in front of a mirror, focusing on precise articulation.

Another set of letters that may cause confusion are "b" and "v" because they have similar pronunciation. Both sounds are produced by the lips, but "b" is more explosive, while "v" is softer and continuous. It's important to learn to distinguish between these two letters to avoid misunderstandings during communication.

Pronunciation exercises are crucial in learning Spanish. You can use various materials such as recordings, movies, or audiobooks to practice correct pronunciation of words and sentences. With regular practice, your pronunciation will become increasingly fluent and natural.

Remember that proper pronunciation is essential for comprehension and effective communication. As you progress in learning Spanish, engage in conversations with native speakers to gain confidence and refine your skills. Be patient and don't get discouraged by difficulties – over time, your pronunciation will improve, and learning Spanish will become more rewarding.

2. Tonic Accent

Tonic accent plays a crucial role in the Spanish language as it distinguishes the meaning of words and influences the flow and melodicity of speech. In each word, only one syllable is accented, while the others are pronounced with less vocal emphasis. To correctly accentuate words and maintain fluency in speech, it's essential to pay attention to some rules regarding tonic accent.

In Spanish, there are specific accentuation rules that can be applied to most words. In most cases, the tonic accent falls on the penultimate syllable of the word if it ends with a consonant, "n," or "s." However, if the word ends with a vowel, "e," or "o," the tonic accent falls on the last syllable.

Examples:

– Árbol (tree) – accent falls on the first syllable "Ár"

– Cárcel (prison) – accent falls on the first syllable "Cár"

– Estudiante (student) – accent falls on the penultimate syllable "Es–tu–dian–te"

In the case of one–syllable words, the tonic accent is usually determined by the sentence context. Some of these words may be accented to emphasize the meaning of the sentence.

Examples:

– No (no) – accented to express firm disagreement: "¡No lo hagas!" (Don't do it!)

– Sí (yes) – accented to confirm something: "Sí, entiendo" (Yes, I understand)

As in any language, there are exceptions to accentuation rules that should be remembered. Sometimes the accent may change depending on the word variant or grammatical form.

Regular listening and repetition exercises of words with different tonic accents will help you master correct pronunciation and accentuation in Spanish. Listen to videos, podcasts, read aloud, and engage in conversations with native speakers to gain confidence and fluency in communication. I encourage regular practice, as mastering the tonic accent is crucial for effective and natural communication in the Spanish language.

3. Listen and Repeat

Improving your pronunciation in Spanish is crucial for effective communication. To enhance your pronunciation, listen carefully to recordings from various sources, focusing on accents and intonation. Repeat Spanish words and sentences, trying to imitate their sounds and melody. Regular practice will bring visible results, making your communication more fluent and confident. Patience and perseverance are key to mastering Spanish pronunciation.

4. Practice Speaking Aloud

Speaking aloud is a crucial element in perfecting your pronunciation in Spanish. Regular exercises will help you develop fluency and self–assurance in communication. Focus on pronouncing different words, sentences, and dialogues to practice various sounds and the melody of the language.

Practice speaking aloud and clearly in solitude or with a language partner. You can use educational materials, audiobooks, movies, or TV shows in Spanish. Listen and imitate the accent and intonation of native speakers, trying to blend into the natural rhythm of the language.

5. Learn Phonetics

Understanding Spanish phonetics will also help you recognize differences in pronunciation between words that may appear similar at first glance. It's essential to familiarize yourself with various recordings from native speakers to improve your phonetic skills. Practice accentuating the right syllables in words, which is crucial in Spanish, where tonic accent plays a significant role. Remember that regular exercises and engagement in phonetic learning will yield significant results in improving your pronunciation and language fluency.

6. Utilize Available Resources

Using a variety of educational materials is crucial in perfecting your pronunciation and accent in Spanish. You can benefit from language textbooks that include pronunciation exercises and audio recordings to familiarize yourself with the correct sound of words. Mobile apps with recording features will allow you to track your progress and self–assess during speaking exercises.

Additionally, listening to Spanish broadcasts such as movies, podcasts, or songs will help your ear get accustomed to different accents and intonations. It's also worth exploring online educational resources where you can find recordings from native Spanish speakers to imitate authentic sounds. Remember the importance of regular practice, as consistent exercises are key to achieving fluency and precision in Spanish pronunciation.

7. Practice with a Partner

Practicing with a language partner is an excellent opportunity to improve your pronunciation and accent in Spanish. Joint exercises will provide mutual support and correction of any errors. Dialogue practice, role–playing, and asking each other questions will allow you to actively practice the language in real communication situations. Conversing in Spanish with a partner will help your ear adapt to authentic language sounds and adjust your accent. Organizing language exchanges with native Spanish speakers will also provide valuable experience and knowledge about the culture and customs of Spanish–speaking countries. Practicing with a partner will help you gain confidence in speaking and develop communication skills in various situations. Remember that consistency and commitment are key to effectively refining your pronunciation and accent.

Chapter 2: At the Hotel and Airport

During your trip to a Spanish–speaking country, booking a hotel room and checking in on–site are crucial steps that will ensure your comfortable stay. To facilitate these tasks, it's beneficial to familiarize yourself with useful phrases and expressions that will allow you to communicate effectively with hotel staff. With them, you'll be able to easily make reservations, understand information about room availability and services, and successfully check–in, saving time and avoiding potential misunderstandings. In this chapter, you'll find examples of sentences and phrases that will be useful in these specific situations, allowing you to enjoy a seamless stay in a Spanish–speaking hotel. *¡Disfruta tu estancia! (Enjoy your stay!)*

Room Reservation and Check–In at the Hotel

1. Room Reservation

– *¿Tiene habitaciones disponibles?* – *Do you have available rooms?*

– *¿Hay habitaciones para hoy?* – *Are there rooms available for today?*

– *Quisiera reservar una habitación individual / doble.* – *I would like to book a single / double room.*

– *¿Cuál es el precio por noche?* – *What is the price per night?*

– *¿El desayuno está incluido en el precio?* – *Is breakfast included in* the price?

– ¿A qué hora es el check–in y el check–out? – What time is check–in and check–out?

– ¿Tienen habitaciones con vista al mar? – Do you have rooms with a sea view?

– Queremos una habitación con aire acondicionado. – We want a room with air conditioning.

– ¿Cuánto cuesta la habitación por una semana? – How much does the room cost for a week?

– ¿Aceptan tarjetas de crédito? – Do you accept credit cards?

– ¿Hay wifi en las habitaciones? – Is there wifi in the rooms?

Hotel Check–In

– Tengo una reserva a nombre de [tu nombre]. – I have a reservation under the name [your name].

– Aquí tiene mi pasaporte / documento de identidad. – Here is my passport / ID card.

– ¿Dónde está mi habitación? – Where is my room?

– ¿Cómo puedo llegar al ascensor / escaleras? – How can I get to the elevator / stairs?

– ¿Dónde está el ascensor? – Where is the elevator?

– ¿A qué hora sirven el desayuno? – What time is breakfast served?

– No me gusta este cuarto, ¿puedo ver otro? – I don't like this room, can I see another one?

3. Additional Information

During your trip to a Spanish–speaking country, making hotel room reservations and checking–in on–site may require attentiveness and knowledge of appropriate phrases. Before arriving, it's advisable to explore various accommodation options and book your room in advance to avoid availability issues.

At the time of check–in, remember to present your identification document, as it is often required by hotels. Additionally, some Spanish–speaking countries may apply a "tasa de turismo" (tourist tax) that needs to be paid upon check–in.

Polite and courteous communication with hotel staff will make your stay more pleasant. Learning basic phrases and expressions will help you ask for information or assistance, allowing you to enjoy the hotel's amenities comfortably and have a successful stay.

Remember, learning Spanish is a process that requires patience and regular practice. Utilize various educational materials, apps, and engage in conversations with native speakers to improve your language skills.

Questions about availability and services at the hotel

During your stay at the hotel, you may have various needs and inquiries regarding the availability of different services. Here are some useful phrases that will help you easily inquire about the offered services at the hotel:

– *¿Hay acceso a Internet Wi– Fi en las habitaciones? – Is there Wi–Fi access in the rooms?*

– *¿Tienen servicio de lavandería? – Do you have laundry service?*

– *¿A qué hora se sirve el desayuno / almuerzo / cena? – What time is breakfast/lunch/dinner served?*

– *¿Tienen servicio de habitaciones? – Is room service available?*

– *¿Cuál es el horario de la piscina / gimnasio / spa? – What are the pool/gym/spa hours?*

– *¿Ofrecen servicio de transporte al aeropuerto? – Do you offer airport transportation service?*

– *¿Hay aparcamiento disponible? – Is there parking available?*

– *¿Tienen habitaciones para no fumadores? – Do you have non–smoking rooms?*

– *¿Cuáles son las atracciones turísticas cercanas? – What are the nearby tourist attractions?*

– *¿Dónde puedo encontrar información turística? – Where can I find tourist information?*

– *¿Cuál es la contraseña del wifi? – What is the Wi–Fi password?*

Do not hesitate to ask questions about any services you need. The hotel staff is there to assist you and make your stay as comfortable as possible. Remember that polite and courteous communication with the hotel staff always yields positive results.

Assistance at the airport and travel–related expressions

Traveling to the airport and using aviation services can be stressful at times, but with the appropriate knowledge of the Spanish language, you can handle all questions and situations more easily. Here are some useful phrases and expressions to help you during your journey.

1. At the airport

– *¿Dónde está la sala de embarque? – Where is the boarding gate?*

– *¿Dónde puedo facturar mi equipaje? – Where can I check in my luggage?*

– *¿Cuál es el número de vuelo? – What is the flight number?*

– *¿A qué hora sale / llega mi vuelo? – What time does my flight depart / arrive?*

– *¿Hay retraso en el vuelo? – Is there a delay in the flight?*

– *¿Dónde está la puerta de salida? – Where is the exit gate?*

– *¿Cuál es la puerta de salida para el vuelo a Madrid? – What is the departure gate for the flight to Madrid?*

2. During security check

– *¿Necesito mostrar mi pasaporte?* – *Do I need to show my passport?*

– *¿Dónde puedo poner mis pertenencias?* – *Where can I put my belongings?*

– *¿Necesito quitarme los zapatos?* – *Do I need to take off my shoes?*

– *¿Puedo llevar esta botella de agua?* – *Can I take this bottle of water?*

– *¿Tengo que sacar mi computadora de la mochila?* – *Do I need to take my computer out of my backpack?*

– *¿Cuánto tiempo llevará el proceso de seguridad?* – *How long will the security check process take?*

– *¿Dónde puedo recoger mis pertenencias después del control de seguridad?* – *Where can I collect my belongings after the security check?*

3. Onboard the plane

– *¿Puedo tener una manta / almohada?* – *Can I have a blanket / pillow?*

– *¿Hay opciones vegetarianas en el menú?* – *Are there vegetarian options on the menu?*

– *¿Cuándo servirán la comida?* – *When will the meal be served?*

– *¿Cuánto durará el vuelo?* – *How long will the flight last?*

– *¿A qué hora llegaremos a nuestro destino? – What time will we arrive at our destination?*

– *¿Dónde están los baños? – Where are the restrooms?*

– *¿Puedo tener otra bebida? – Can I have another drink?*

4. After arrival at the destination

– *¿Dónde puedo recoger mi equipaje? – Where can I collect my luggage?*

– *¿Hay transporte público desde el aeropuerto? – Is there public transportation from the airport?*

– *¿Dónde puedo encontrar un taxi? – Where can I find a taxi?*

– *¿A qué hora cierra la oficina de alquiler de coches? – What time does the car rental office close?*

– *¿Cuánto tiempo lleva llegar al centro de la ciudad desde aquí? – How long does it take to get to the city center from here?*

– *¿Puedo dejar mi equipaje en una consigna? – Can I leave my luggage in a locker?*

– *¿Dónde está la oficina de información turística? – Where is the tourist information office?*

– *¿Cómo llego a la estación de tren desde aquí? – How do I get to the train station from here?*

Remember that there's nothing wrong with asking questions and seeking help. The airport staff is there to assist you and ensure your journey is as comfortable as possible. Practicing these expressions will help you feel more confident and at ease while traveling in Spanish–speaking countries.

Chapter 3: Communication and Transportation

In this chapter, we will focus on essential skills that will help you travel comfortably in a Spanish-speaking country. You will learn how to find appropriate means of transportation, purchase tickets, and ask questions about schedules. You will also learn how to communicate with taxi drivers, bus, and train conductors, and gain practical tips for using public transportation. Welcome to the fascinating world of communication and transportation in a Spanish-speaking country. Good luck on your journey!

Finding the Right Means of Transportation

During your travels in a Spanish-speaking country, it's important to know how to inquire about various means of transportation, such as buses, taxis, and trains, as well as how to ask for information about their schedules and routes. Learning the appropriate phrases will allow you to have a smooth and enjoyable journey in a Spanish-speaking country.

1. Questions about buses

– *¿Dónde puedo tomar el autobús a [destination]? – Where can I catch the bus to [destination]?*

– *¿Cuándo sale el próximo autobús? – When does the next bus leave?*

– ¿El autobús llega al centro de la ciudad? – Does the bus go to the city center?

– ¿Cuántas paradas hay hasta [destination]? – How many stops are there to [destination]?

– ¿Cuál es la siguiente parada? – What is the next stop?

– ¿Me puede indicar dónde bajar para ir al museo? – Can you tell me where to get off to go to the museum?

– ¿Tengo que hacer alguna escala o cambio de autobús? – Do I have to make any transfers or change buses?

– ¿Cuánto tiempo tengo para hacer la conexión? – How much time do I have to make the connection?

– ¿Este autobús va a [destination]? – Does this bus go to [destination]?

2. Questions about trains

– ¿Dónde está la estación de tren? – Where is the train station?

– ¿A qué hora sale el próximo tren a [destination]? – What time does the next train to [destination] leave?

– ¿Dónde puedo encontrar el horario de los trenes? – Where can I find the train schedule?

– ¿Cuánto tiempo lleva llegar a [destination] en tren? – How long does it take to get to [destination] by train?

– ¿Puedo abrir la ventana? – Can I open the window?

Chapter 4: Dining in Restaurants and Cafes

During your travels to Spanish-speaking countries, one of the most enjoyable experiences is tasting the local cuisine. Restaurants and cafes are an integral part of the Spanish culture, where you can try unique dishes and savor aromatic coffee. In this chapter, we will familiarize ourselves with useful phrases and expressions that will help you effectively order meals, ask about the menu, and request the bill and service. Additionally, we will learn how to inquire about local specialties and make the most of valuable recommendations from waiters to make our culinary experience exceptional. *¡Buen provecho! (Enjoy your meal!)*

Ordering in a Restaurant and Asking About the Menu

When you are in a Spanish-speaking country and want to eat at a restaurant, it's important to know basic phrases related to placing an order and asking about the menu. Here are some useful expressions that will help you in your culinary adventures:

- *¿Tiene menú del día? – Do you have a daily menu?*

- *¿Cuál es la especialidad de la casa? – What is the house specialty?*

- *¿Qué platos vegetarianos tienen? – What vegetarian dishes do you have?*

- *Para mí, [dish name]. – For me, [dish name].*

– *Quisiera [dish name], por favor.* – *I would like [dish name], please.*

– *De primer plato, tomaré la sopa. Y de segundo plato, el pescado.* – *For the first course, I'll have the soup. And for the second course, the fish.*

– *¿Me puede traer la carta de vinos, por favor?* – *Could you bring me the wine list, please?*

– *Sin cebolla, por favor.* – *Without onion, please.*

– *Con papas fritas en lugar de ensalada.* – *With French fries instead of salad.*

– *¿Puede poner la salsa aparte?* – *Can you serve the sauce on the side?*

– *Eso es todo, gracias.* – *That's all, thank you.*

– *Nada más, gracias.* – *Nothing else, thank you.*

Using these phrases will make your dining experience in Spanish–speaking countries more enjoyable and help you communicate your preferences to the restaurant staff.

Requests for the Bill and Service

When you finish your meal at a restaurant, it's time to ask for the bill and conclude your visit. Here are some useful phrases related to requesting the bill and expressions related to service:

– *La cuenta, por favor.* – *The bill, please.*

– *¿Nos trae la cuenta, por favor? – Could you bring us the bill, please?*

– *Queremos pagar, por favor. – We would like to pay, please.*

– *¿Aceptan tarjetas de crédito? – Do you accept credit cards?*

– *¿Se puede pagar en efectivo? – Can we pay in cash?*

– *¿Tienen terminal para pagos con tarjeta? – Do you have a card payment terminal?*

– *Gracias por el servicio. – Thank you for the service.*

– *El servicio fue excelente. – The service was excellent.*

– *¿Nos puede traer una botella de agua, por favor? – Could you bring us a bottle of water, please?*

– *Creo que hay un error en el rachunek. – I think there's a mistake in the bill.*

– *Disculpe, no pedimos esto. – I'm sorry, we didn't order this.*

– *Falta un plato en el rachunek. – There's a dish missing on the bill.*

– *¡Gracias y hasta luego! – Thank you and see you later!*

– *¡Ha sido una comida deliciosa! – It was a delicious meal!*

– *¡Esperamos volver pronto! – We hope to come back soon!*

Chapter 5: City Sightseeing

During your travels to a Spanish-speaking country, exploring the city provides a unique opportunity to discover its rich history, culture, and attractions. In this chapter, we will focus on discovering fascinating places, asking the right questions about key tourist attractions to make the most of our journey. Additionally, we will learn how to use maps and navigation to easily navigate through the city and avoid getting lost. We won't forget practical aspects such as finding restrooms and other public facilities to ensure comfort during our sightseeing. Let's embark on this journey to the most beautiful corners of Spanish-speaking cities and enjoy unforgettable experiences! *¡Vamonos! (Let's go!)*

Asking about Key Places to Visit

During our travels, it's not just about the flavors, but also about exploring the culture and beauty of the place. Here are some useful questions to help you find out about the most important attractions to visit:

1. General Questions about Tourist Attractions

– ¿Cuáles son los lugares más visitados de la ciudad? – What are the most visited places in the city?

– ¿Qué sitios turísticos recomienda visitar aquí? – What tourist sites do you recommend visiting here?

– ¿Dónde están los principales puntos de interés? – Where are the

main points of interest located?

2. Questions about Monuments and Museums

– ¿Hay algún castillo o monumento histórico que no deba perderme? – Is there a castle or historical monument that I must not miss?

– ¿Cuál es el museo más interesante de la ciudad? – What is the most interesting museum in the city?

– ¿Cuáles son los sitios históricos más importantes de la región? – What are the most important historical sites in the region?

3. Questions about Nature and Landscapes

– ¿Dónde puedo disfrutar de las vistas panorámicas más impresionantes? – Where can I enjoy the most breathtaking panoramic views?

– ¿Cuáles son los parques naturales más bonitos de la zona? – What are the most beautiful natural parks in the area?

– ¿Hay alguna playa o montaña cercana que valga la pena visitar? – Are there any beaches or mountains nearby that are worth visiting?

4. Questions about Cultural Events and Festivals

– ¿Hay algún evento especial o festival que se celebre durante mi estancia? – Are there any special events or festivals taking place during my stay?

– ¿Cuándo y dónde puedo disfrutar de espectáculos folklóricos o

conciertos locales? – When and where can I enjoy folkloric performances or local concerts?

5. Questions about Relaxation and Entertainment

– ¿Cuáles son los mejores lugares para salir por la noche? – What are the best places to go out at night?

– ¿Dónde puedo encontrar los restaurantes más auténticos con comida local? – Where can I find the most authentic restaurants serving local food?

– ¿Hay algún centro comercial o mercado donde pueda comprar recuerdos y souvenirs? – Is there any shopping center or market where I can buy souvenirs and gifts?

Remember that when you ask about places to visit, you may receive many valuable tips from locals who know the best hidden treasures of their region. Have fun exploring new places and cultures!

Tips for Using Maps and Navigation

Traveling in a foreign country can be very exciting but also challenging if you're not familiar with the area. Here are some useful tips to help you use maps and navigation during your journey:

1. Choose the right map

Make sure you're using an up-to-date map of the region or city. You can use a traditional paper map or smartphone apps that offer GPS navigation.

2. Check your location

Always check your location on the map to get a sense of your surroundings. Compare the map view with what you see in reality to ensure you're heading in the right direction.

3. Mark important landmarks

Identify landmarks on the map, such as distinctive buildings, squares, or main streets, to help you navigate the area more easily.

4. Utilize GPS navigation

If you're using a smartphone app or GPS navigation, ensure that the location feature is enabled. This will help pinpoint your exact location and track your route.

5. Follow step–by–step instructions

When using GPS navigation, choose the step–by–step directions option to receive precise guidance from point A to point B. In some areas, GPS signal may be weak, especially in mountainous regions or large buildings. In such cases, it's helpful to have a traditional map as a backup plan.

6. Ask for help

If you have doubts or get lost, don't hesitate to ask locals for directions. People are often willing to assist and can point you in the right direction.

7. Prepare in advance

Before you head out, check the route and major places you want to visit. Familiarize yourself with street names and locations to navigate the area more effectively.

Finding Restrooms and Other Public Facilities

During your travels, regardless of whether you're in a big city or a smaller town, it's important to know where to find restrooms and other public facilities. In larger cities and tourist areas, you can easily find public restrooms at train stations, shopping centers, and parks. If there are no available public restrooms, you can use facilities in cafes, restaurants, or gas stations. Remember to take care of your own supply of toilet paper in case there's none provided in public restrooms. Avoid relieving yourself in public places, following local customs and rules. Here are some sentences to help you with this issue:

- *¿Dónde está el baño más cercano? – Where is the nearest restroom?*

- *¿Hay baños públicos aquí? – Are there any public restrooms here?*

- *Disculpe, necesito ir al baño. – Excuse me, I need to use the restroom.*

- *¿Dónde puedo encontrar un baño limpio? – Where can I find a clean restroom?*

- *¿Hay algún baño disponible para los clientes? – Are there any restrooms available for customers?*

- *¿Puede indicarme dónde están los servicios? – Can you show me* *where the restrooms are?*

– ¿Hay baños aquí cerca? – Are there restrooms nearby?

– Perdón, ¿dónde se encuentra el baño para discapacitados? – Excuse me, where is the restroom for people with disabilities?

– ¿Dónde puedo lavarme las manos? – Where can I wash my hands?

– ¿Hay algún lugar para cambiar pañales? – Is there a place to change diapers?

– ¿Cuánto cuesta usar el baño aquí? – How much does it cost to use the restroom here?

– ¿Tienen papel higiénico en el baño? – Do you have toilet paper in the restroom?

Chapter 6: Shopping and Bargaining

When traveling to a Spanish–speaking country, shopping and bargaining are not only important aspects of the culture but also a great opportunity to discover local products and traditions. In this chapter, we will explore useful phrases and tips for asking about prices and product availability, mastering the art of bargaining, and obtaining information about store hours and markets. By acquiring these skills, your shopping experiences will not only be more enjoyable but will also help you better understand the local culture of trade and communication. Let's begin our journey into the shopping world of the Spanish–speaking country! *¡Buenas compras! (Happy shopping!)*

Asking about prices and product availability

When traveling to a Spanish–speaking country, you may want to find out about the prices and availability of various products. Here are some useful phrases to help you ask for this information:

– *¿Cuánto cuesta esto? – How much does this cost?*

– *¿Tienen esto en otros colores/tallas? – Do you have this in other colors/sizes?*

– *¿Tienen descuentos especiales? – Do you have any special discounts?*

– *¿Cuánto tiempo se tarda en preparar esto? – How long does it take to prepare this?*

– *¿Tienen este producto en stock? – Do you have this product in stock?*

– *¿Hay alguna oferta especial? – Is there any special offer?*

– *¿Aceptan tarjetas de crédito? – Do you accept credit cards?*

– *¿Cuál es el precio final? – What is the final price?*

– *¿Puedo obtener un descuento si compro más de uno? – Can I get a discount if I buy more than one?*

– *¿Cuál es el precio más bajo que pueden ofrecer? – What is the lowest price you can offer?*

It's worth noting that bargaining in shops is not as common as in some other countries. In most shops and service points, prices are fixed, but in some places, you can try to ask for a better offer, especially if you plan to make larger purchases.

When asking about prices and product availability, it's essential to speak clearly and use a polite tone. This way, you show respect for the local culture and increase your chances of getting accurate information.

Remember that exploring local products and price lists can be a fascinating experience during your travels. With the use of these phrases, you will be able to converse freely with local shopkeepers and discover the diversity of products offered in the places you visit.

Bargaining and price negotiations

Bargaining and price negotiations are often present at local markets, bazaars, and some shops in Spanish–speaking countries. It is an essential part of the shopping culture that can bring a lot of satisfaction to travelers. Here are a few tips to help you effectively bargain for a price:

1. Start with a proposal

Propose a price that is lower than what you are willing to pay. Remember that the initial value should be reasonable but also leave room for potential concessions.

2. Be polite

Words can get heated during negotiations, but remember to maintain politeness and respect. It is important in the culture of Spanish–speaking countries.

3. Learn some useful phrases

– *¿Cuál es tu mejor precio? – What is your best price?*

– *¿Me puedes hacer un descuento? – Can you give me a discount?*

– *Es demasiado caro. – It's too expensive.*

– *¿Cuál es tu último precio? – What is your final price?*

4. Be flexible

Try to negotiate in a flexible and open–minded way. It will help you find a mutually beneficial solution.

5. Find common ground

Focus on finding a point where both parties will be satisfied with the final price.

6. Don't be afraid to walk away

If you can't reach an agreement on the price, don't be afraid to thank the seller and walk away. In some cases, it may lead the seller to change their mind and accept a lower price.

7. Enjoy the game

Remember that bargaining is a kind of game and fun, so enjoy it and keep an open mind.

It's also essential to remember that not all places and situations require bargaining. In some shops or markets, prices are fixed, and negotiations are not appropriate. It's always worth observing the behavior of local people and adapting your approach accordingly.

Bargaining and price negotiations can be an exciting and rewarding experience during your travels. It also provides an opportunity to get closer to the local culture and traditions. Remember that shopping at local markets is not just a way to acquire unique souvenirs but also a chance to interact with local residents and discover the authentic beauty of the place.

Questions about the opening hours of shops and the bazaar

When traveling to Spanish–speaking countries, it's essential to know the opening hours of shops, bazaars, and other commercial places. The schedule may vary depending on the region and the type of establishment, so it's worth asking the right questions to plan your shopping and sightseeing. Here are some useful phrases and questions regarding opening hours:

– *¿A qué hora abren? – What time do you open?*

– *¿A qué hora cierran? – What time do you close?*

– *¿A qué hora abre el mercado? – What time does the market open?*

– *¿A qué hora cierra la tienda de souvenirs? – What time does the souvenir shop close?*

– *¿Cuál es el horario de apertura? – What is the opening schedule?*

– *¿Cuál es el horario de cierre? – What is the closing schedule?*

– *¿Está abierto los domingos? – Is it open on Sundays?*

Remember that opening hours may vary depending on the day of the week and circumstances, such as holidays or festivals. Therefore, it's always worth verifying the information and ensuring that the place you want to visit will be open at that time.

It's also essential to pay attention to the Spanish siesta tradition, especially in some regions. Often, at noon, many shops, restaurants, and other businesses close for a few hours to allow employees and customers to rest and relax. It's a good opportunity to take a break yourself, take advantage of the time to rest, or visit a local market or bazaar known for its unique products and atmosphere.

Additionally, if you need help understanding the answers to questions about opening hours, it's worth learning basic numbers in Spanish and days of the week. It will facilitate communication and planning during your travels.

Remember that flexibility and readiness to adjust plans are crucial during travel. Sometimes shops or markets may have variable opening hours, but this flexibility can lead to unforgettable discoveries and adventures during your journey. Have fun and enjoy your adventure in Spanish–speaking countries!

Chapter 7: Emergencies and Assistance

While traveling, no matter how well-prepared we are, unexpected situations can arise that require our attention and action. In this chapter, we will focus on topics related to safety and health while traveling. You will learn how to deal with lost luggage, how to call for help in emergencies, and how to take care of your health in a foreign country. Familiarize yourself with useful phrases and tips that will help you stay calm and confident in unexpected situations. *¡Prioriza tu seguridad y bienestar! (Prioritize your safety and well-being!)*

Reporting Lost Luggage

During your travels, unfortunately, situations like lost luggage can occur. It's essential to know the steps to take in such situations and how to report the problem effectively. Here are some useful phrases and tips for reporting lost luggage and emergencies:

– ¿Dónde puedo reportar un equipaje perdido? – Where can I report lost luggage?

– He perdido mi maleta. – I lost my suitcase.

– ¿Cuál es el procedimiento para reportar un equipaje perdido? – What is the procedure for reporting lost luggage?

– Necesito completar un formulario de reclamación. – I need to complete a claim form.

– ¿Pueden ayudarme a localizar mi equipaje? – Can you help me locate my luggage?

– ¿Cuánto tiempo suele tomar encontrar el equipaje perdido? – How long does it usually take to find lost luggage?

In case of lost luggage, make sure to contact the appropriate authorities and personnel, such as airport staff, as soon as possible. Notify them about the situation and provide as much information as possible to help resolve the issue.

It's crucial to remain calm in such situations and provide all necessary information to ensure a swift processing of your report. Follow the recommendations and instructions from the relevant authorities and personnel.

By keeping these tips in mind, you will be better prepared for potential situations during your travels and be able to effectively handle any issues that may arise. Remember that safety and appropriate action are essential during your journey.

Summoning Help and Contacting Local Emergency Services

During your travels, whether you are in a city or in the countryside, there is always a risk of situations that require assistance or support from local emergency services. In the event of a sudden accident or emergency, it is essential to know how to summon the appropriate help. Here are some useful phrases and tips for calling for help and contacting local emergency services:

1. Calling an Ambulance

– *Ha ocurrido un accidente. – An accident has occurred.*

– *¿Necesito llamar a una ambulancia? – Do I need to call an ambulance?*

– *¡Ayuda! ¡Llamen a un médico! – Help! Call a doctor!*

– *Ha habido un choque en la carretera. – There has been a crash on the road.*

– *¿Dónde está la estación de policía más cercana? – Where is the nearest police station?*

– *¿Hay un hospital cercano? – Is there a hospital nearby?*

– *¡Necesito una ambulancia! – I need an ambulance!*

– *¡Llame al número de emergencia! – Call the emergency number!*

– *Alguien está herido. – Someone is injured.*

– *¿Dónde puedo encontrar un teléfono para llamar al 112 (or appropriate emergency number in the country)? – Where can I find a phone to call 112 (or appropriate emergency number in the country)?*

2. Contacting the Police

– *¿Dónde está la comisaría de policía más cercana? – Where is the nearest police station?*

– *¡Necesito reportar un robo! – I need to report a theft!*

– Ha ocurrido un incidente y necesito ayuda de la policía. – An incident has occurred, and I need police assistance.

– ¿Puede ayudarme a contactar a la policía? – Can you help me contact the police?

– ¿Cuál es el número de emergencia de la policía local? – What is the emergency number for the local police?

Remember, in case of emergencies, it's crucial to stay calm and provide clear and accurate information to the local authorities or emergency services. Being familiar with the local emergency numbers and knowing how to ask for help will help you react promptly and effectively in case of unexpected situations during your travels.

3. Calling the fire brigade

– ¡Llame a los bomberos! – Call the fire brigade!

– Hay un incendio en el edificio. – There's a fire in the building.

– ¿Dónde está el hidrante más cercano? – Where is the nearest fire hydrant?

– ¡Necesitamos ayuda para apagar el fuego! – We need help to extinguish the fire!

– ¿Cuál es el número de emergencia de los bomberos? – What is the emergency number for the firefighters?

In case of calling for help or contacting local emergency services, it's important to provide as accurate information as possible about the situation, such as the address, type of incident, or the number of people injured. Remember that in emergencies, time is crucial, so it's worth familiarizing yourself with the appropriate emergency numbers in the country you're traveling to and always have them at hand during your journey. By acting appropriately and quickly, you can help yourself and others in crisis situations.

Health and Safety While Traveling

During your travels, it's important to take care of your health and safety to fully enjoy the experiences. Here are some tips regarding health and safety while traveling:

1. Prepare a travel first aid kit

– Pack essential medications such as painkillers, fever reducers, anti–diarrheal medicine, band–aids, and disinfectants.

– Check if you need any vaccinations before traveling to a specific country and consult your doctor if you have any doubts.

2. Travel insurance

– Purchase travel insurance that covers medical expenses and medical evacuation if needed.

– Ensure the policy covers all the activities you plan to do during your trip, such as extreme sports or diving.

3. Practice good hygiene

– Wash your hands regularly with soap and water, especially before eating.

– Avoid drinking untreated water and use bottled water for drinking.

4. Street safety

– Exercise caution on the streets and avoid dangerous areas, especially at night.

– Always carry a copy of your travel documents and leave the originals in a safe place at your hotel.

5. Precautionary measures during travel

– Stick to main tourist routes and avoid unknown, isolated places.

– Don't leave your luggage unattended, especially at airports and train stations.

6. Take care of your mental health

– Long journeys and changes in environment can be stressful. Remember to take breaks and care for your mental well–being.

– Find time for meditation, reading, or other relaxing activities to unwind during your travels.

Remember, you can take care of your health and safety by planning and preparing before your trip. Knowledge about your destination and basic precautions will help you enjoy your journey without unnecessary worries. If needed, always seek assistance from local medical services or your country's consulate. Above all, have fun, explore new places and cultures while ensuring your health and the safety of yourself and others.

Chapter 8: Useful Apps and Resources

In today's world, traveling has become easier thanks to advanced technology. In this chapter, we will focus on useful apps and resources that can help you during your travels to Spanish-speaking countries. You will learn about various language-learning apps that will enable you to communicate and interact in a foreign country. Additionally, you'll discover practical websites and guides that provide valuable information about places to visit, culture, and traditions of the region. Moreover, you'll find offline dictionaries and translators for your phone, serving as invaluable tools when you don't have internet access. Equipped with these resources, your journey will become even more exciting and enjoyable, allowing you to explore new places and interact with the local community without language barriers. Prepare yourself for unforgettable experiences and make the most of modern resources every step of the way on your adventure through Spanish-speaking countries. *¡Aprovecha al máximo tu viaje! (Make the most of your trip!)*

Apps for Learning Spanish While Traveling

In today's world, technology is an invaluable aid in learning foreign languages, including Spanish. When planning your trip to a Spanish-speaking country, it's worth utilizing various mobile apps that can help you quickly master the basics of the language and communicate with ease during your travels. Here are a few popular apps to consider:

1. Duolingo

Duolingo is one of the most popular language–learning apps. It offers interactive lessons that teach grammar, vocabulary, and pronunciation in a fun and effective way.

2. Babbel

Babbel is another popular app that provides Spanish language courses at various proficiency levels. You can learn through interactive lessons and dialogues.

3. Memrise

Memrise is an app that relies on the method of memorization through repetition. It offers a rich database of words and phrases that can be quickly internalized through a spaced repetition system.

4. Rosetta Stone

Rosetta Stone is an advanced language–learning app that utilizes the immersion technique, enabling you to gain fluency in communication quickly.

These apps will undoubtedly enhance your language skills and make your journey more enjoyable and fulfilling.

5. HelloTalk

HelloTalk is a unique app that allows you to practice language in real–time through conversations with native speakers. You can find language exchange partners who want to learn your language while you learn Spanish from them.

6. Tandem

Tandem is another language–learning app that enables conversations with native speakers. You can find a language partner for tandem learning and exchange language skills.

7. Anki

Anki is a flashcard app for language learning. You can create your own flashcards with Spanish words and review them regularly.

8. FluentU

FluentU is a platform that uses authentic video materials for learning Spanish, such as movies, TV shows, and music videos.

9. SpanishDict

SpanishDict is an app for quick translations, grammar reference, and pronunciation. It's perfect for immediate assistance during your travels.

10. SpeakEasy

SpeakEasy is an app for learning essential phrases and expressions needed while traveling. It will help you quickly master communication in various situations.

Some of these apps are available for free, while others may require a subscription, but investing in learning Spanish for your trip will undoubtedly pay off. Choose the ones that best suit your needs and learning style, and you'll be ready for smooth communication in a Spanish–speaking environment during your adventure abroad.

Practical Websites and Guides for Travelers

In the age of the Internet, traveling has become much easier due to access to practical information, tips, and online guides. When planning a trip to a Spanish–speaking country, it's worth using various websites and guides that can help you plan and organize your journey. Here are some useful sources:

1. TripAdvisor (www.tripadvisor.com)

TripAdvisor is one of the most popular websites where travelers share their opinions about hotels, restaurants, tourist attractions, and other places. You can find valuable tips from other travelers.

2. Booking.com (www.booking.com)

Booking.com is a platform that allows you to book accommodations online. You'll find a wide selection of hotels, hostels, and apartments in various locations.

3. Skyscanner (www.skyscanner.net)

Skyscanner is a flight search engine that enables you to compare airfares across different airlines and find the cheapest flights.

4. Lonely Planet (www.lonelyplanet.com)

Lonely Planet is one of the most renowned travel guide publishers, offering detailed information about various countries and cities, including Spanish–speaking regions.

5. Rough Guides (www.roughguides.com)

Rough Guides is another popular travel guide series providing comprehensive information about different destinations worldwide, including Spain and other Spanish–speaking countries.

6. Spain.info (www.spain.info)

Spain.info is the official tourism portal of Spain, where you can find information about major tourist attractions, cultural events, and other aspects of traveling in Spain.

7. WordReference (www.wordreference.com)

WordReference is one of the best online dictionaries and language forums, where you can find translations of words and phrases from Spanish to many other languages.

8. Wikitravel (www.wikitravel.org)

Wikitravel is a free travel encyclopedia where you can find practical information about various places worldwide, including Spanish–speaking countries and cities.

9. Spain–Holiday (www.spain–holiday.com)

If you plan to rent an apartment or house in Spain, this website offers many accommodation options in different regions of the country.

10. Eat Spain Up! (www.eatspainup.com)

If you're interested in Spanish cuisine, this website is a treasure trove of information about traditional dishes, local delicacies, and the best places to eat.

It's beneficial to use various online sources and guides to obtain comprehensive information and tips for traveling to Spanish–speaking countries. Remember that each traveler has different preferences and needs, so choose the websites and guides that best align with your expectations and travel plans.

Dictionaries and Offline Translators on Your Phone

When traveling to a Spanish–speaking country, it's essential to have access to a good dictionary and translator that can help you communicate and understand the local language. Nowadays, thanks to advanced technology, you can have these tools at your fingertips even without internet access. Here are some recommended offline dictionaries and translators for your phone:

1. Duolingo

We already mentioned this app for language learning, but it also includes an offline dictionary and translator feature. You can download the appropriate language pack before your trip and have access to translations without needing an internet connection.

2. SpanishDict

SpanishDict is one of the best apps for learning Spanish. You can download the offline dictionary, which includes definitions, translations, sample sentences, and many other useful pieces of information.

3. Google Translate

Google's Translate app offers an offline feature, allowing you to download language packs and use translations without an internet connection.

4. Dict.cc

Although primarily known as a German dictionary, Dict.cc also offers translations to and from Spanish. You can download the offline dictionary and use it during your travels.

5. Spanish English Translator

This app provides translations from Spanish to English and vice versa. You can download the offline package and use it without internet access.

6. Reverso

Reverso is an app that offers translations, definitions, and usage examples of words and phrases. You can download the offline dictionary and use it while traveling.

7. iTranslate

iTranslate is an advanced translator that offers translations to and from many languages, including Spanish. You can download the offline dictionary and use it during your journey.

It's a good idea to have several different dictionaries and translators installed on your phone because different apps offer various features and include different vocabulary. Also, make sure to download the appropriate language packs before your trip to use the offline translations. With these apps, you'll be able to communicate confidently during your travels and navigate the Spanish–speaking environment more easily. The mentioned apps are available for both Android and iOS.

Chapter 9: Traveling with Confidence

Congratulations! You've successfully reached the end of our practical guide "Spanish for Travel." I hope this book has been helpful to you and has allowed you to communicate with ease during your travels to Spanish-speaking countries.

Throughout the guide, you have learned many basic polite forms and greeting phrases that are essential for initiating first contact with locals in Spain, Mexico, Colombia, or any other Spanish-speaking country. You have also learned how to ask questions about names, origins, and the purpose of your trip, enabling you to engage in interesting conversations and get to know new people better.

Furthermore, you have acquired the ability to understand simple answers to questions and express brief statements on various travel-related topics. You have also learned practical phrases and expressions useful for booking hotel rooms, using public transportation, and ordering meals in restaurants.

Thanks to this guide, you have also gained knowledge about using maps and navigation in unfamiliar places, finding public restrooms and other facilities, and handling various crisis situations during your travels.

Don't forget about the practical apps and offline dictionaries on your phone that will allow you to freely translate and understand Spanish during your journey.

I hope that the skills you have acquired will enable you to fully enjoy your adventurous journey in a Spanish–speaking country and establish interesting and inspiring connections with local residents. Wishing you safe travels and many wonderful experiences! *A disfrutar del viaje! (Enjoy your journey!)*